PERMIS

IMPOSSIBLE

METAL DETECTING SEARCH
PERMISSION MADE EASY

David Villanueva

Published by True Treasure Books
www.truetreasurebooks.net

ISBN-13: 978-0-9550325-3-0

Copyright © David Villanueva 2007
Reprinted 2011, 2017

CONTENTS

ACKNOWLEDGMENTS

My grateful thanks go to all those who have been kind enough to provide their ideas and input to this book, particularly: Josh Kimmel, Noel Pearce, Brian Port

1 INTRODUCTION

The biggest problems facing the metal detecting hobby today are undoubtedly finding productive land and securing search permission. My book *Site Research,* (Greenlight Publishing, 2006), deals extensively with the quest for productive land through map, local history and document research. Research in itself will always help secure search permission by effectively answering the landowner's question: Why do you want to search my land? What's more you are almost guaranteed good finds once you obtain permission. So site research is a very good way of improving your chances of obtaining permission, which I will cover later along with many other tips and techniques designed to multiply your land portfolio.

As the new chairman of a metal detecting club, which over the years had become a 'landless society', I was charged with the task of finding land for the club to search. This is where things can get difficult. Many landowners will willing give permission to one or two detectorists to search but facial contours distort somewhat when you say: "And will it be OK if I bring twenty mates along?" I skirt around this problem for the club by saying 'as few as one or two of us' and if that is the agreement then the club can run a rota system so that all can share eventually in the 'reduced number searches'. One other potential problem with clubs is the amount of cars that turn up for a search. Car sharing doesn't seem to go down well with detectorists and this can be a problem for a farmer. Please make sure it isn't or you probably will not be visiting that farm again.

Let's now take a look at the reasons search permissions are refused. The biggest reason used to be the non-committal: we don't allow that sort of thing. Today, in my area, Kent, the most often quoted reason is that: we already have a couple of detectorists on our land. As well as still not allowing that sort of thing, another reason might be that the occupier is a tenant and in that case, the tenant will usually co-operate if you get permission from the landowner.

Our task here is not to try and oust other detectorists from land they have diligently obtained permission to search and any attempts at that may result in everyone being banned from that particular land. But rather to work around other detectorists' patches by seeking out productive land where permission can be relatively easily obtained or no other detectorist treads, for whatever reason.

One very important point is that you absolutely MUST work tidily. There is little point in making the effort of getting permission only to have it withdrawn because you are making a mess and putting the whole hobby into disrepute as well. So wherever you are searching field, beach, garden you must leave the site as you found it with all holes filled in and extracted rubbish removed. If the land is used by domestic animals such as livestock or horses the consequences of leaving unfilled holes could be tragic. Landscaped areas such as gardens and parks need special attention and aim for invisible extractions. Use a straight-edged trowel to cut a neat plug with three or four sides approximately 200mm (8") long. Cut the plug with sloping sides to help its keying in when you replace it. Lift out the plug, invert it and place it on a sheet of polythene, cloth or Frisbee so that loose dirt and the plug can be put back into the hole, the same way it came out, without leaving a brown halo on the surrounding grass. In very dry weather the grass will die back after being disturbed so either water the grass after find extraction (you may need to carry a bottle of water with you) or only search these places when the ground is damp. So now let's go to it and happy hunting!

2 THIS LAND IS MINE

Your own land in the UK, is the only place where you have a right to use a metal detector, and not even there, if your land happens to be defined as a Scheduled Monument or a Site of Special Scientific Interest. For most of us our own land will consist of a garden of some sort, which is nevertheless a very good place to start. Gardens will have seen much human activity in a relatively small area: gardening, sunbathing, alfresco meals, children playing, etc. Not to mention the possibility of metallic losses from whatever took place before the garden was laid out. I remember finding over 50 coins in my mother-in-law's 1920s garden and my most valuable single find, a Tudor iconographic gold ring, came from the garden of a 13th century house. So check out your garden and any other land you or your family owns or rents perhaps, although strictly you should obtain permission from the landowner if searching rented land. However if you are the occupier of the land as in the case of a garden or you have an allotment for instance, the landowner is unlikely to object. You may only be looking for your own lost possessions there, after all.

Having searched your own land you will have a few finds to show and will undoubtedly be able to find relatives, friends, neighbours and work-mates willing to allow you to search their land also for a share in the finds. This simple approach of asking anyone and everyone you know could keep you busy with sites for quite some time.

Throughout the UK there are around NINE MILLION properties

and parcels of land which haven't been registered. While a lot of this land will be visibly in use and most will have an owner somewhere, there is still an enormous acreage of run down or derelict farms and buildings, overgrown fields and hidden plots which you may be able to make use of for metal detecting. I will show you how to make enquiries at the Land Registry in a later chapter and if you find the land is unregistered you may even be able to claim it as your own through Adverse Possessory Title. That is a job for a solicitor though, not for this book.

The ideal place to start looking for these properties, as with any land for metal detecting, is in your own neighbourhood and you will find it easier to spot these places on foot or bicycle rather than in a car. If you find a likely looking plot of land, you ought to make enquiries of the Land Registry and elsewhere (see chapter: Tracking Down Landowners) before doing anything else. The snag is that by definition, the land will be derelict, overgrown or have had rubbish dumped on it and generally not be searchable as it stands. However if the land would be worth searching with a metal detector it would probably be worth clearing, which may not be too big a problem for a club. Depending on the nature of the site it may be 'all hands to the pumps' or even feasible to hire machinery or a contractor to mow, level, plough or whatever. For the individual this may not be so easy, however, claiming the land, clearing it, searching it and selling it off later could well be worth the trouble and expense.

3 MAKE FOR THE COAST

While searching beaches and tidal rivers isn't everyone's cup of tea, they are places where you can generally metal detect either without the formality of obtaining permission or, in some cases, you can buy a permit to search. While, there are many beaches and foreshores (the foreshore is defined as: the area between mean high and mean low water (spring tides in Scotland)) in private ownership, the usual 'ownership' is local Council above high water mark and Crown below.

The Crown Estates had a free permit system, now suspended (keep checking their website) and you are currently free to use a metal detector on foreshores in England, Northern Ireland, Scotland and Wales under their control, providing you follow a few simple rules set out on the Crown Estates website: https://www.thecrownestate.co.uk/rural-and-coastal/coastal/metal-detecting/
Email: enquiries@thecrownestate.co.uk/

Write: The Crown Estate, Marine Department, 16 New Burlington Place, London, W1S 2HX

In Scotland, the Outdoor Access Code gives everyone a statutory right of access to beaches, foreshores and the countryside, for outdoor pursuits, apparently including responsible metal detecting, so no permit is necessary. There are obviously a number of restrictions such as cultural heritage and archaeological sites, so check out:

http://www.outdooraccess-scotland.com/outdoors-responsibly/your-access-rights/

For the river Thames, the Port of London Authority effectively owns the foreshore and runs a three-year permit system, for metal detecting between Teddington and the Thames Barrier. The current fee is £75.00 (day permit: £32). See the National Council for Metal Detecting Website: http://www.ncmd.co.uk/ for conditions and an application form. Applications to: Mr K Jackelman, Port of London of Authority, London River House, Royal Pier Road, Gravesend, Kent DA12 2BG. Email: foreshorepermits@pla.co.uk/ Tel: 01474 562339.

Public beaches are usually accessible for metal detecting, however local bylaws must be adhered to for the sake of the hobby. Bylaws will usually restrict detecting to early mornings and evenings during the holiday season. This is for the benefit of all beach users and, whether bylaws exist or not, you shouldn't be searching with a metal detector around sunbathers and others enjoying the beach, unless you have been asked specifically to find some newly lost property. It is just bad manners as well as being a very inefficient way to search.

Private beaches where the public has free access are usually equally accessible for metal detecting as the public variety, (although strictly you should seek permission from the owner). In many cases you won't be able to tell the difference. However, do look out for notices, which may affect access or searching. Private, Keep Out! Means just that, unless you obtain permission and bear in mind the restriction may be because of danger. Ministry of Defence (MOD) property is a case in point.

Some beaches and foreshores are designated a Site of Special Scientific Interest (SSSI) or similar, and while metal detecting is prohibited on such sites inland, it is usually allowed on the foreshore and beaches barren of plant life, subject to non-interference with flora or fauna and protective structures such as dunes. Check with Natural England, if in doubt. The National Trust (or regional equivalents) owns a number of beaches and will not usually allow metal detecting without a good reason. However, they will seldom own the entire beach and foreshore so it is quite possible to work around their area of ownership, provided you find out, from e.g. Ordnance Survey maps, what area they own. Some hotels own beaches for the enjoyment of their guests. You may be able to gain permission out-of-season and you could offer to search for guests' lost property in-season.

The situation with non-tidal waterways or watercourses is somewhat different. A landowner with frontage along a watercourse is presumed to own the bed up to the centre of the watercourse. Clearly if the same landowner owns both banks then he owns the entire bed, unless there is contrary proof. Sometimes errors in conveyance occur and the bed is not transferred with the land, sometimes beds are bought and sold separately. The usual case with working canals and some rivers is that ownership is vested in the navigation authority, by Act of Parliament, to facilitate control over the use of the waterway.

While detecting non-tidal watercourses does require permission from the landowner, notwithstanding the rights of other users such as anglers, permission may be easier to obtain than that on the surrounding land. Not only that, like beaches and foreshores, watercourses are potentially a year round site and benefit from replenishment.

In my early days in this hobby I used to mainly detect beaches and usually stayed on the dry sand where there were a great many coin and jewellery losses to be found. As time went on gangs of local detectorists tied up the most productive beaches and farmland became more attractive as detector technology improved. Most fields used to be ploughed annually, ensuring a new crop of finds each year and land was left for relatively long periods before drilling, allowing searching for several months. Today, economic pressures on farming have reduced ploughing to a minimum, drilling taking place a few days after harvesting from the back of a cultivator. Now there's a new game afoot – direct drilling into stubble! The result is a much shorter detecting season on farmland. I am dedicated to all year round detecting so I have been investigating foreshores like never before as that's generally where the older losses lie and what's more, the tides refresh the sites twice daily. The last foot and mouth epidemic well and truly brought the potential of tidal foreshores home to me. On farmland I was finding Celtic, Roman, Saxon, Medieval and modern coins and artefacts, the epidemic relegated me to the beach and with a little research into maps, charts and local histories, I was coming home with exactly the same range of objects, Celtic to modern. So, when all your productive fields are under crop or otherwise unavailable, don't be a stick-in-the-mud, do a little research on any beaches, tidal rivers or inland waterways you can get to and keep bringing home the finds. That's what I'm doing these days.

4 SEARCH AND RECOVERY SERVICE

It is a good idea to offer a free search and recovery service for lost 'valuables'. This may not only gain you access to sites, you would not normally be able to search, such as private gardens, but it may lead to search permission to all manner of sites, large and small. And don't forget the greatest hoard of Roman gold and silver yet found in Britain was recovered in Hoxne by detectorist Eric Lawes looking for a farmer's lost hammer! We don't know if he found the hammer but the £1.75 million treasure trove award would buy a mountain of replacements!

Of the 'valuables' you could offer to look for, keys and jewellery are probably the most valuable. The cost of recovering from losing a bunch of keys can run into hundreds of pounds, in replacement locks and damage caused breaking into lockers, briefcases, filing cabinets, etc. Not to mention the worry that someone might have found the keys and be up to no good with them. And a single item of Jewellery can be worth thousands of pounds and/or of great sentimental value.

Farmers, in particular, are very good at losing tools and parts of tractors, combine harvesters and the like. Also the burying of manholes, drain covers and stopcocks, which then need to be uncovered, seems to be a national sport.

On the next page is a copy of a club advert for a search and recovery service. You can design your own or copy the example on the page following, adding your name(s) and phone number(s) in the blank space to the right of the lower ring. Take your adverts to all libraries and police stations within the area you can comfortably cover (e.g. a 20-mile radius) and ask them if they will display your advert or at least keep it behind the desk for future reference. Depending on where you live, there may be many other opportunities for you to advertise your service for free, lost property offices, hotels, caravan sites, camping sites, tourist information offices, community centres, park offices, sporting clubs, supermarket notice boards, etc. You can also, if you wish, pay to advertise in newsagents and other shops who place notices in their windows.

Once you start getting enquiries, it's up to you to make the most of the opportunity. If you quickly locate what you have been asked to look for, you could ask if you might continue searching the site for a half-share of non-personal finds. Lost property always belongs wholly to the legal owner and you are not entitled to any payment or reward unless you have made a prior agreement with the owner. If you are offered a reward, it is up to you whether you accept or not, depending on circumstances. My inclination would be to decline, saying I enjoyed the search and did they know of any other land where I might get permission to use my detector.

The finding of a drain cover won't generate much interest in the local press but a jewellery recovery of great intrinsic or sentimental value, or any unusual recovery, undoubtedly will. So, with the grateful owner's agreement, contact the local newspaper and give them the story. This is always great free publicity for you and your hobby and will bring more searches and more detecting permissions as well.

David Villanueva

IF YOU'VE LOST

**KEYS, JEWELLERY, TOOLS, MACHINE
PARTS, DRAIN COVERS; IN FACT
ANYTHING METAL OR PART METAL**

ON ANY OPEN SPACE: GRASS, SOIL, BEACH, ETC.

AND YOU KNOW ROUGHLY WHERE

0123 456789

<u>FREE</u> SEARCH AND RECOVERY SERVICE

IF YOU'VE LOST

KEYS, JEWELLERY, TOOLS, MACHINE PARTS, DRAIN COVERS; IN FACT ANYTHING METAL OR PART METAL

ON ANY OPEN SPACE: GRASS, SOIL, BEACH, ETC.

AND YOU KNOW ROUGHLY WHERE

<u>FREE</u> SEARCH AND RECOVERY SERVICE

5 TRACKING DOWN LANDOWNERS

It always helps a great deal when seeking search permission if you can address your request to the landowner by name. If nothing else it shows you have done your homework.

The easiest place to start is the classified section of the telephone directory; www.192.com/ Yellow Pages; www.yell.com/ Thompsons; www.thomweb.co.uk/ etc. You can get access to printed directories outside of your telephone area at your local library and online directories cover the entire UK. A typical search would be for farmers in a locality defined by name of nearest town or city or first half of postcode. If you have more information such as name of farm, address, etc. you may be able to perform a more selective search.

There are a couple of points here. The entry does not necessarily list the name of the current landowner, some farms have business names and those with personal names may date from the 19th century. For farms with personal names, if you can't get any closer to the current landowner's name, then if you use Mr. (surname) you will be OK much of the time. For farms having business names you could address letters to the landowner or chief executive and start: Dear Sir. However this is not very satisfactory and you would be better to pursue other avenues to find the name of the landowner. The second point is that the names and addresses of these farms are public knowledge and many detectorists in the area have probably already tried them, so if you are approaching them without a good reason, expect to be turned down.

Another method of finding the landowner, particularly useful for fields with no obvious farmhouse attached, is to visit the area and ask people living or working in the immediate vicinity. You could also ask at the local church, local shops or businesses, post office, newsagent or public house.

Everyone entitled to vote is recorded on the Electoral Roll or Electoral Register, which can be very useful providing the landowner lives on the premises and has not elected to be excluded from the Public Register. The current Public Register is kept at the local council office and anyone is entitled to inspect it free of charge. It is best to telephone the council offices beforehand and find out which office(s) holds the register and what the procedure is for consulting it. My local council allows inspection on demand but other councils may run an appointment system, for instance. I haven't been asked why I wanted to look at the Electoral Register and you probably won't be either but there is nothing wrong in wanting to find the name of a landowner, after all it may be to his advantage too.

The Register is organised by Ward then by street then by postcode but there is a street name index, so providing you know which road (look at https://www.google.co.uk/maps/ or an A-Z street map) the property is in or near, then it will be quite easy to find it in the Register. Once you have found the entry for the property the household will be listed in alphabetical order of name. If there are only one or two people listed, it is usually fairly obvious who is the head of the family. You would normally pick the male unless only females are listed. Larger families need a bit of deduction applied. Older names like Amos are likely to be more senior than Elvis. Anyone who was a minor when the Register was compiled will have a date in brackets against their name. If you can't decide on who the head of family is you can simply address the landowner as Mr. or Ms. (surname).

Moving on to the slightly more involved, when all else fails there is the Land Registry, who, since 1990, are obliged to give out details to anyone enquiring about title to land and property on the Register. This may involve a little form filling and fees, however. The process can be a little involved so, for England and Wales, it is probably best to start by getting a free copy of Land Registry **Public Guide 1**, *A Guide to the Information We Keep and How You Can Obtain It,* or the more recent: **Practice guide 10:** *official search of the index map,* which contain much useful information on the register, forms, etc. Guides can be obtained by post from: Land Registry Citizen Centre, PO Box 74, Gloucester GL14 9BB. Or download from the Internet at https://www.gov.uk/government/organisations/land-registry/ All forms you might need can be downloaded from the website or obtained by post from the Gloucester Office at the above address. If you can't find what you want on the website home page, continue to the forms and publications pages.

Land in Scotland is dealt with by Registers for Scotland, Customer Service Centre, Meadowbank House, 153 London Road, Edinburgh, EH8 7AU. http://www.ros.gov.uk/ Tel: 0800 1699391. There is a public search facility, which works somewhat differently to England and Wales. For Northern Ireland, only registers from 1990 are currently searchable without a landowners' name: https://www.finance-ni.gov.uk/topics/land-registration/registry-deeds/ Customer Information Centre, Lanyon Plaza, 7 Lanyon Place, Town Parks, BELFAST, BT1 3LP.

In England and Wales, there are basically two scenarios, where the Land Registry can help. The first is when the property can be identified by a single postal address. This simply involves filling in Form **OC1**, and sending it, along with a small fee, to the Land Registry office. Or do it online at: www.landregistry.gov.uk/ Be aware that there are similarly titled commercial sites charging much higher fees.

Your most likely need for the Land Registry will be to find land with no obvious postal address or farmhouse, especially as the trend nowadays is for many smaller farms to be bought up by larger concerns, with the landowner living miles away from the land you are interested in. This is a slightly more complex exercise in form filling so I will cover that in some detail. You will need forms **SIM** and **OC1** from the Land Registry Citizen Centre or their website (addresses above). The guides mentioned may also prove useful, as will **Information services fees.**

Form **SIM** is an application for an official search of the index map. Fill in as much information as you can about the property. Although **SIM** is only for an index check to find the title number for the next stage, there is a fee required with this form (£5.00 in 2011). You will also need to attach a copy of a modern Ordnance Survey map with the land highlighted or outlined in a colour, which stands out. You can get a copy of the relevant map from the local public library or www.bing.com/maps/ Coloured highlighters, pens or pencils can be used to define the area of land you are interested in, just describe how you are showing the land in panel 6 on the form. E.g. 'edged in blue'; 'coloured yellow'. Finally sign and date the form.

If you are able to work with a computer the easiest and cheapest route is to send the **SIM** and attachments off and wait for the Land Registry to supply the postcode and title number, usually by return of post. You should then have sufficient information to complete form **OC1** on line and submit it for a reduced fee. This enables you to download the Register for that property, which will include the name and address of the proprietor or landowner.

On the following pages there is an example of a completed **SIM** form.

Land Registry
Application for an official search of the index map

	LAND REGISTRY USE ONLY
If you need more room than is provided for in a panel, and your software allows, you can expand any panel in the form. Alternatively use continuation sheet CS and attach it to this form.	Record of fees paid
Land Registry is unable to give legal advice but our website www1.landregistry.gov.uk provides guidance on Land Registry applications. This includes public guides and practice guides (aimed at conveyancers) that can also be obtained from any Land Registry office.	Particulars of under/over payments
See www1.landregistry.gov.uk/regional if you are unsure which Land Registry office to send this application to.	Reference number Fees debited £

Where there is more than one local authority serving an area, enter the one to which council tax or business rates are normally paid.	**1**	Local authority serving the property: **CANTERBURY CITY COUNCIL, KENT**
If no postal address insert description, for example 'land adjoining 2 Acacia Avenue'	**2**	Property to be searched
		Flat/unit number
		Postal number or description: **LAND AT WEST SIDE OF WRAIK HILL, FORMERLY PROSPECT HOUSE FARM**
		Name of road: **WRAIK HILL**
		Name of locality
		Town: **WHITSTABLE**
		Postcode:
		Ordnance Survey map reference (if known): **TR101645**
		Known title number
	3	Application and fee

Application	Fee paid (£)
Search of the index map	**£5.00**

See fees calculator at www1.landregistry.gov.uk/fees

Place 'X' in the appropriate box.

The fee will be charged to the account specified in panel 4.

Fee payment method

X cheque made payable to 'Land Registry'

☐ Land Registry credit account

☐ direct debit, under an agreement with Land Registry

4	This application is sent to Land Registry by
If you are paying by direct debit, this will be the account charged.	Key number (if applicable):
	Name: **DAVID VILLANUEVA** Address or UK DX box number **2 DARN CLOSE, WHISTABLE, KENT AB1 2CD** Email address: **DAVID@TRUETREASUREBOOKS.COM** Reference: **W05**
	Phone no: 0123 456789 | Fax no:

Please note that the facility of issuing results electronically is not available at present. When it is, a direction will appear on our website and details will be given in Public Guide 1 and Practice Guide 10. Until there is a direction, you do not need to complete this panel to obtain an official copy in paper format. Official copies issued electronically are in 'Portable Document Format' (PDF) which replicates the appearance of the hard copy version. You will need Adobe Acrobat Reader (which you can install free from www.adobe.com) to open the document. Place 'X' in the box if applicable.	5	Issue of certificate of result of search in paper format where an email address has been supplied If you have supplied an email address in panel 4, then, unless you complete the box below, any certificate of result of search of the index map will be issued electronically to that address, if there is a direction under section 100(4) of the Land Registration Act 2002 by the registrar covering such issuing. ☐ I have supplied an email address but require the certificate of result of search to be issued in paper format instead of being issued electronically
Any attached plan must contain sufficient details of the surrounding roads and other features to enable the land to be identified satisfactorily on the Ordnance Survey map. A plan may be unnecessary if the land can be identified by postal description.	6	I apply for an official search of the index map in respect of the land referred to in panel 2 shown **EDGED IN BLUE** on the attached plan
	7	Signature of applicant: _Dc Villan_ Date: 05 10 11

WARNING
If you dishonestly enter information or make a statement that you know is, or might be, untrue or misleading, and intend by doing so to make a gain for yourself or another person, or to cause loss or the risk of loss to another person, you may commit the offence of fraud under section 1 of the Fraud Act 2006, the maximum penalty for which is 10 years' imprisonment or an unlimited fine, or both.

Failure to complete this form with proper care may result in a loss of protection under the Land Registration Act 2002 if, as a result, a mistake is made in the register

Under section 66 of the Land Registration Act 2002 most documents (including this form) kept by the registrar relating to an application to the registrar or referred to in the register are open to public inspection and copying. If you believe a document contains prejudicial information, you may apply for that part of the document to be made exempt using Form EX1 under rule 136 of the Land Registration Rules 2003.

© Crown copyright (ref LR/HO) 07/08

If you are not into computers or online payments, together with the **SIM** form and map, you need to submit a completed **OC1** form. Start by writing: 'PLEASE SUPPLY THE TITLE NUMBER' in capital letters on the top of the form. Fill in the details of the land (property) as before in panels 1 & 3. Put an X in the box for 'freehold estate' in panel 2. Overleaf, you require ONE official copy of the register (panel 7) and also put ONE as the total number in panel 4. Note here that there is a further fee, which is £8.00 (2011) but check with the Land Registry or website for current fees. Record the fee paid and put X in the box for cheque or other payment method. Make out separate cheques payable to the Land Registry and attach them to the **SIM** and **OC1** forms. If the Land Registry can't supply the information they will return at least one of your cheques. Fill in your name and contact details in panel 5. On the third page in panel 8 I suggest you put an X in the lower box so you get the official copy on completion of any pending application. Sign and date the form in panel 9.

Put everything in an envelope addressed to the Land Registry Citizen Centre, affix the correct postage and pop it in the post. Within a week or so you should receive either a copy of the register with the landowner's details or a note saying the land isn't registered, together with at least some of your fee returned. An example of a completed **OC1** form follows:

Land Registry
Application for official copies of register/
plan or certificate in Form CI

OC1

PLEASE SUPPLY THE TITLE NUMBER

Use one form per title.

If you need more room than is provided for in a panel, and your software allows, you can expand any panel in the form. Alternatively use continuation sheet CS and attach it to this form.

Land Registry is unable to give legal advice but our website www1.landregistry.gov.uk provides guidance on Land Registry applications. This includes public guides and practice guides (aimed at conveyancers) that can also be obtained from any Land Registry office.

See www1.landregistry.gov.uk/regional if you are unsure which Land Registry office to send this application to.

LAND REGISTRY USE ONLY
Record of fees paid
Particulars of under/over payments
Reference number / Fees debited £

Where there is more than one local authority serving an area, enter the one to which council tax or business rates are normally paid.

Use a separate form for each registered title.

Place 'X' in the appropriate box.

1 Local authority serving the property
CANTERBURY CITY COUNCIL, KENT

2 Details of estate
(a) Title number if known:
(b) (Where the title number is unknown) this application relates to
X freehold ☐ leasehold ☐ manor
☐ franchise ☐ caution against first registration
☐ rentcharge ☐ profit a prendre in gross

3 Property

Flat/unit number:

Postal number or description: **LAND AT WEST SIDE OF WRAIK HILL, FORMERLY PROSPECT HOUSE FARM**

Name of road: **WRAIK HILL**

Name of locality:

Town: **WHITSTABLE**

Postcode:

4	Application and fee		
	Application	Total number of all copies or certificates requested in panel 7	Fee paid (£)
	Official copy of register /plan or certificate of inspection of title plan	ONE	8.00

See fees calculator at www1.landregistry.gov.uk/fees

Fee payment method

Place 'X' in the appropriate box.

The fee will be charged to the account specified in panel 5.

X   cheque made payable to 'Land Registry'

☐   Land Registry credit account

If you are paying by credit account or direct debit, this will be the account charged.

☐   direct debit, under an agreement with Land Registry

5	This application is sent to Land Registry by

Key number (if applicable):

Name: **DAVID VILLANUEVA**
Address or UK DX box number:
2 DARN CLOSE WHITSTABLE KENT AB1 2CD

Email address: **DAVID@TRUETREASUREBOOKS.COM**
Reference: **W05**

Phone no: **0123 456789**	Fax no:

Please note that the facility of issuing copies electronically is not available at present. When it is, a direction will appear on our website and details will be given in Public Guide 1 and Practice Guide 11. Until there is a direction, you do not need to complete this panel to obtain an official copy in paper format.

Official copies issued electronically are in 'Portable Document Format' (PDF) which replicates the appearance of the hard copy version. You will need Adobe Acrobat Reader (which you can install free from www.adobe.com) to open the document.

Place 'X' in the box if applicable.

6	Issue of official copies in paper format where an email address has been supplied

If you have supplied an email address in panel 5, then, unless you complete the box below, any official copy will be issued electronically to that address, if there is a direction under section 100(4) of the Land Registration Act 2002 by the registrar covering such issuing.

☐   I have supplied an email address but require the official copy(ies) to be issued in paper format instead of being issued electronically

Indicate how many copies of each are required.

7	I apply for

ONE official copy(ies) of the register of the above mentioned property

____   official copy(ies) of the title plan or caution plan of the above mentioned property

Place 'X' in the appropriate box.

____   certificate(s) of inspection of title plan, in which case either

i. ☐   an estate plan has been approved and the plot number is:

or

State reference, for example 'edged red'

ii. ☐   no estate plan has been approved and a certificate is to be issued in respect of the land shown on the attached plan and copy

Land Registry forms are Crown copyright and are reproduced by kind permission of Land Registry.

6 THE PLANNERS

There is another way that landowners' names and addresses become publicly available and that is whenever a landowner makes a planning application, regardless of the outcome. This can cover all sorts of property and projects from a modest householder building a garage, through lords building staff accommodation and farmers erecting new buildings, to major housing or industrial developments.

Getting metal detecting permission on building sites is fraught with difficulties owing not only to health and safety issues but also the risk of increased costs and hold-ups if an important archaeological discovery is made. However, some planning applications, such as demolition, tree surgery and sign erection do not involve construction. Also the planning application may fail or be withdrawn and even construction projects may have considerable areas of land outside the actual building works where permission to detect may be forthcoming. So keeping an eye on planning applications is a worthwhile pursuit if only to build up a database of landowners for possible future use.

Planning is the responsibility of local authorities who must make the details of all planning applications available to the public. This is principally to allow anyone to object or comment on the content. The procedure does vary slightly around the country, however the information will be available and accessible. As usual it is always best to start with an area that you know.

If you know the name of the local authority you can look them up in the telephone directory (local libraries keep a wide range of directories) or type name + planning in an Internet search engine. If you don't know who the local authority is, there is a search facility on the Planning Portal website: www.planningportal.gov.uk/ or you can ask directory enquiries for the town hall or council offices, who will then put you in touch with planning.

All planning authorities must publish a Planning Register and are legally obliged to make this available to the public. Applications are normally published weekly, however the register goes back to 1974 so if you spot a fairly recent structure on land that interests you, you can often get the landowner's details from the associated application months or years previously. You can consult this register at the planning department office and it may be available elsewhere: council offices, libraries and certainly on the Internet. While the Internet is the most convenient for computer users, the amount of information available may be limited. Even so you should be able to obtain the applicant's name and address for recent applications, although this will not necessarily be the landowner as sometimes an agent is used, whose name and address is given. You could still contact the landowner for search permission via the agent, however. If you need more information than is available on the Internet you will have to visit the planning department office, where you will normally find the staff very helpful, owing to their legal obligation to the public.

Typically the Planning Register will contain the following information:

Application number:

Application type:

Registration Date:

Comments welcome by:

Committee date:

Location: (address of property)

Ward:

Proposal: (the intended work)

Case Officer: (for council)

Case Officer Tel:

Status:

Registered Agent:

Applicant: (property owner or agent (if name and address is same as registered agent))

Decision:

Appeal Received Date:

In addition there will be other associated documentation, sometimes available online, e.g.

Application Form

Associated Documents

Plans/Drawings

Site Plan

7 WRITING A LETTER AND GETTING IT READ

I have met a few detectorists with the ability to knock on any landowner's door for the first time and sweet talk him or her into unconditional permission. If you have that ability, carry on! You probably won't need much of this chapter. For the rest of us with the philosophy: the meek shall inherit the earth, if the rest of you don't mind, it is a very different story and writing is usually the best way to avoid being traumatised or ending up with a flea in the ear. Writing has the advantage of introducing yourself and your hobby at the recipient's leisure, giving him a chance for a considered reply, rather than a knee-jerk no! If the landowner feels strongly negative, then a quick note returned to that effect avoids a potentially unpleasant confrontation. Some landowners will respond positively almost immediately but the majority, and this is the downside of letter writing, will not respond at all and you won't know why, at the time.

One reason for lack of response could be that your letter was never read. This may be because your letter is illegible or unintelligible or was never received or not opened. We can and should take steps to maximise the chances of our letter being read.

Firstly a hand written letter will probably be the best received PROVIDING IT IS COMPLETELY AND EASILY READABLE. You should know how well you own penmanship is received, if not, ask anyone who does not know your writing well to assess an example. If someone takes a sample of my handwriting into the chemist they come out with a bottle of aspirins. If your writing is like that – forget it! You must type or word-process your letters, or have someone do that for you. If you don't have the wherewithal to do that task yourself try relatives, friends, colleagues or find someone under Secretarial Services in the Yellow Pages.

Unless you are making a financial proposition to the landowner, business type letter headings are best avoided. Club letter headings are generally acceptable and perhaps unavoidable. Later I will be discussing other letters but meanwhile a typical letter might be laid out as the example on the next page. Save your letter if you have produced it on a word processor, otherwise make a copy of the letter and keep it.

Put the letter in an envelope with minimal folding. Enclose a first-class (which implies urgency) stamped self-addressed envelope, a copy of the Code of Practice or NCMD Code of Conduct and copies of maps and any other printed material that supports your argument for wanting to search the land. Indicate on the map where you want to search if it isn't obvious. Affix postage stamps to the correct first class postage rate. Avoid labels or franking as this may make your letter look like a circular and get it relegated to the bin.

Post the letter and wait. You will often get a fairly quick yes. If you haven't heard from the landowner by the end of four weeks, visit him, if possible, taking a copy of your letter and any research with you. You are not 'cold calling' so he should be approachable and he is unlikely to be completely against the idea or he would already have replied to that effect. You will just have to try and convince him to say yes even if it is only for a short probationary period.

If you can't get to see the landowner send another brief letter suggesting you think the first may have been lost in the post and enclose a copy of the original letter with copies of everything you originally sent, including a stamped self-addressed envelope.

Permission Impossible

Your name
Your address
Your telephone number
Your email address (if you have one)

(Date)

(Landowner's title) (Landowner's Surname)
(Landowner's Address)

Dear *(Title e.g. Mr) (Surname)*,
   Several years ago a local farmer kindly gave me permission to use a metal detector on his land. The finds recovered, from the top <u>few inches</u> of soil (coins, tokens, buttons, buckles and a variety of other metal artefacts that had been lost, hidden or discarded over the past 2000 years) led me to develop a considerable interest in the history of the area.
   During the course of research I have come across several references to a Roman road that is supposed to have run through *(name)* parish. According to major sources (e.g. Ordnance Survey Map of Roman Britain) the road ran from the Iron working area of *(name)* through *(name)* to *(name)*, where it crossed the river and travelled up the east side to *(name)*. It looks highly probable that the road continued on from *(name)* to *(name) Street*, crossing your land. It is, perhaps, worth noting that Roman finds have been made on nearly all adjoining fields.
   I would greatly appreciate having your permission to use a metal detector on your land with a view to determining the course of the Roman road
   In return for your kind permission, I offer to:
1) Report all worthwhile finds and findings to you.
2) Share any finds or their value with you on the customary 50/50 basis.
3) Work tidily without leaving a mess; removing all junk uncovered.
4) Respect your property and take care to avoid causing damage, loss or hindrance (I have N.F.U./C.L.A. approved Public Liability Insurance).
5) Abide by any conditions that you wish to impose.
   I am at your disposal should you require further information or a demonstration and look forward to your reply.

Yours Sincerely,

(Your Signature)
Enc: SAE, Code of Practice

8 PROPERLY ADDRESSED?

I remember well passing finds around a dining table large enough to seat a couple of football teams, when I was invited in for tea and cake by a Knight and his Lady. Metal detecting is a very interesting hobby and you often find yourself having to write or speak to all manner of people – aristocracy, clergy, businessmen – and many have strong preferences as to how they are addressed. While it is not a criminal offence to get it wrong, it will help your case greatly if you get it right.

I will cover the most likely 'titled' persons you are likely to come across and generally include the correct address for the envelope, the letter opening (Dear:) and how they should be addressed if you need to speak to them. If I haven't covered the situation here you will need to get down to your local library and consult one of the following books:

Burke's Peerage and Baronetage

Debrett's Peerage and Baronetage

Pears' Cyclopaedia

Titles and Forms of Address, (A & C Black)

Webster, Jennifer, *Forms of Address for Correspondence and Conversation*

Whitaker's Almanack

WRITING TO BUSINESSES

Farmers are the most likely businesses you will be dealing with and they are often either one-man-bands or family businesses, so if you have a name, address your letter to that person. With any business you approach, it is always better to try and find out the name of the person who deals with matters relating to company land and how they like to be addressed (Dr., Mr., Mrs., Ms., Miss, etc). A quick phone call to the business concerned will usually establish that and unless it is a very small business you shouldn't get dragged into a conversation about the precise nature of your interest in their land. If you must write without the person's details, address your letter to The Secretary and start your letter: Dear Sirs.

When signing off the letter, if you don't know the addressees name and you start your letter *Dear Sirs*, it is safest to use: *Yours faithfully.* Use: *Yours sincerely* if you address your letter to someone by name. Similarly when writing to titled people other than directly to Royalty or the Pope use: *Yours sincerely* if you know the person personally or *Yours faithfully,* if you don't.

WRITING TO ROYALTY

There's nothing like unbridled ambition is there? If you don't know the member of the Royal Family personally, you should address your letter to his or her Private Secretary asking that the contents of the letter be brought to the attention of *Her Majesty the Queen* or *His Royal Highness, Prince Charles, The Prince of Wales* or *Her Royal Highness, The Duchess of York, etc.* Note that the children of monarchs are *The* Prince and *The* Princess, except when followed by a further *'The'* title, e.g. *His Royal Highness, The Prince Edward* but *Her Royal Highness, Princess Anne, The Princess Royal.*

WRITING TO THE CLERGY

Church of England

POSITION	ENVELOPES	DEAR: (also address as)
Archbishop (current)	The Most Revd. and Rt. Hon. The Lord Archbishop of York (or Canterbury)	Archbishop
Archbishop (retired)	The Most Revd. and Rt. Hon. The Lord Archbishop *Surname*	Archbishop
Bishop of London (current)	The Rt. Revd. and Rt. Hon. The Lord Bishop of London	Bishop
Bishop of London (retired)	The Rt. Revd. and Rt. Hon. The Lord Bishop *Surname*	Bishop
Bishop (current)	The Rt. Revd. The Lord Bishop of *City*	Bishop
Bishop (retired)	The Rt. Revd. The Lord Bishop *Surname*	Bishop
Dean (or Provost)	The Very Revd. the Dean (or Provost) of *Place-name*	Dean (or Provost)
Vicar (or Rector)	The Revd. *Forename Surname*	Vicar (or Rector) or Mr./Mrs./Ms etc. *Surname*

POSITION	ENVELOPES	DEAR: (also address as)
Canon	The Revd. Canon *Forename Surname*	Canon
Archdeacon	The Venerable the Archdeacon of *Place-name*	Archdeacon

Church of Scotland

Clergy	The Revd. *Forename Surname*	Mr./Mrs./Ms etc. *Surname*

Roman Catholic Church

Archbishop (current)	His Grace the Archbishop of *City*	Archbishop *Surname* or (Not Dear) Your Grace
Archbishop (retired)	The Most Revd. Archbishop *Surname*	Archbishop *Surname*
Bishop (current)	His Lordship the Bishop of *Place-name*	Bishop *Surname* or (Not Dear) My Lord
Bishop (retired)	The Rt. Revd. Bishop *Surname*	Bishop *Surname*
Monsignor	The Revd. Monsignor *Forename Surname*	Monsignor *Surname*

POSITION	ENVELOPES	DEAR: (also address as)
Abbot	The Rt. Revd. the Abbot of *Place-name*	Father *Surname* or (Not Dear) Right Reverend Father (Address as Abbot)
Other Priests	The Revd. *Forename Surname*	Father *Surname*

WRITING TO THE ARISTOCRACY

Duke	The Duke of *Place-name*	Duke
Duchess	The Duchess of *Place-name*	Duchess
Widow of duke	The Dowager Duchess of *Place-name*	Duchess
Younger son of duke or marquess (marquis)	Lord *Forename Surname*	Lord *Forename*
Wife of above	Lady ***Lord's Forename*** Surname	Lady ***Lord's Forename***
Daughter of duke or marquess (marquis)	Lady *Forename Surname*	Lady *Forename*
Marquess (Marquis)	The Marquess of *Place-name*	Lord *Place-name*

POSITION	ENVELOPES	DEAR: (also address as)
Earl	The Earl of *Place-name*	Lord *Place-name*
Countess	The Countess of *Place-name*	Lady *Place-name*
Younger son of earl	The Hon. *Forename Surname*	Mr. *Surname*
Wife of above	The Hon. Mrs. **Husband's Forename** *Surname*	Mrs. *Surname*
Daughter of earl	Lady *Forename Surname*	Lady *Forename*
Viscount	The Viscount *Place-name*	Lord *Place-name*
Viscountess	The Viscountess *Place-name*	Lady *Place-name*
Son of viscount or baron	The Hon. *Forename Surname*	Mr. *Surname*
Wife of above	The Hon. Mrs. **Husband's Forename** *Surname*	Mrs. *Surname*
Daughter of viscount or baron	The Hon. *Forename Surname*	Miss *Surname*
Baron	The Lord *Surname*	Lord *Surname*
Wife of baron	The Lady *Surname*	Lady *Surname*

POSITION	ENVELOPES	DEAR: (also address as)
Wife of life peer	The Lady *Surname*	Lady *Surname*
Children of life peer	The Hon. *Forename Surname*	Mr. or Miss *Surname*
Baronet	Sir *Forename Surname* Bt.	Sir *Forename*
Wife of baronet	Lady *Surname*	Lady *Surname*
Knight	Sir *Forename Surname* KBE (or other decoration as applicable)	Sir *Forename*
Wife of knight	Lady *Surname*	Lady *Surname*

9 CODE OF PRACTICE AND CODE OF CONDUCT

A new Code of Practice, a four-page leaflet, was introduced in 2006 and having an impressive list of organisations endorsing it will carry some weight with landowners. Printed copies are available from Finds Liaison Officers (FLOs) and copies can be downloaded from the Portable Antiquities Scheme (PAS) Website: www.finds.org.uk/ or National Council for Metal Detecting website: www.ncmd.co.uk/ The National Council for Metal Detecting (NCMD) Code of Conduct has stood the hobby in good stead for many years and you can use that if you prefer. Both are reproduced on the following pages so you know what I am talking about.

If you don't have computer access the contact details for the PAS and NCMD are as follows:

Portable Antiquities Scheme, The British Museum, London, WC1B 3DG. Tel: 020 7323 8611/8618.

National Council for Metal Detecting, John Rigby, Membership Secretary, 6 Arkholme Avenue, Blackpool, Lancs, FY1 6QJ Tel: 01253 692313. Email: jjrigby@sky.com/ General enquiries: https://www.ncmd.co.uk/contact/

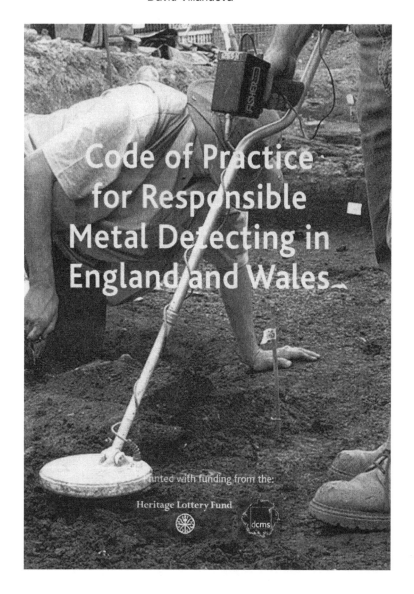

Code of Practice
for Responsible
Metal Detecting in
England and Wales

Printed with funding from the:

Heritage Lottery Fund

dcms

Being responsible means:

Before you go metal-detecting

1. Not trespassing; before you start detecting obtain permission to search from the landowner/occupier, regardless of the status, or perceived status, of the land. Remember that all land has an owner. To avoid subsequent disputes it is always advisable to get permission and agreement in writing first regarding the ownership of any finds subsequently discovered (see www.cla.org.uk / www.nfuonline.com/).

2. Adhering to the laws concerning protected sites (e.g. those defined as Scheduled Monuments or Sites of Special Scientific Interest: you can obtain details of these from the landowner/occupier, Finds Liaison Officer, Historic Environment Record or at www.magic.gov.uk/). Take extra care when detecting near protected sites: for example, it is not always clear where the boundaries lie on the ground.

3. You are strongly recommended to join a metal detecting club or association that encourages co-operation and responsive exchanges with other responsible heritage groups. Details of metal detecting organisations can be found at www.ncmd.co.uk / www.fid.newbury.net/

4. Familiarising yourself with and following current conservation advice on the handling, care and storage of archaeological objects (see www.finds.org.uk/).

While you are metal-detecting

5. Wherever possible working on ground that has already been disturbed (such as ploughed land or that which has formerly been ploughed), and only within the depth of ploughing. If detecting takes place on undisturbed pasture, be careful to ensure that no damage is done to the archaeological value of the land, including earthworks.

6. Minimising any ground disturbance through the use of suitable tools and by reinstating any excavated material as neatly as possible. Endeavour not to damage stratified archaeological deposits.

7. Recording findspots as accurately as possible for all finds (i.e. to at least a one hundred metre square, using an Ordnance

Survey map or hand-held Global Positioning Systems (GPS) device) whilst in the field. Bag finds individually and record the National Grid Reference (NGR) on the bag. Findspot information should not be passed on to other parties without the agreement of the landowner/occupier (see also clause 9).

8. Respecting the Country Code (leave gates and property as you find them and do not damage crops, frighten animals, or disturb ground nesting birds, and dispose properly of litter: see www.countrysideaccess.gov.uk/).

After you have been metal-detecting

9. Reporting any finds to the relevant landowner/occupier; and (with the agreement of the landowner/occupier) to the Portable Antiquities Scheme, so the information can pass into the local Historic Environment Record. Both the Country Land and Business Association (www.cla.org.uk/) and the National Farmers Union (www.nfuonline.com/) support the reporting of finds. Details of your local Finds liaison Officer can be found at www.finds.org.uk/ e-mail info@finds.org.uk/ or phone 020 7323 8611.

10. Abiding by the provisions of the Treasure Act and Treasure Act Code of Practice (www.finds.org.uk/), wreck law (www.mcga.gov.uk/) and export licensing (www.mta.gov.uk/). If you need advice your local Finds Liaison Officer will be able to help you.

11. Seeking expert help if you discover something large below the ploughsoil, or a concentration of finds or unusual material, or wreck remains, and ensuring that the landowner/occupier's permission is obtained to do so. Your local Finds Liaison Officer may be able to help or will be able to advise of an appropriate person. Reporting the find does not change your rights of discovery, but will result in far more archaeological evidence being discovered.

12. Calling the Police, and notifying the landowner/occupier, if you find any traces of human remains.

13. Calling the Police or HM Coastguard, and notifying the landowner/occupier, if you find anything that may be a live explosive: do not use a metal-detector *or* mobile phone nearby as this might trigger an explosion. Do not attempt to move or interfere with any such explosives.

This code of practice is voluntary, but the following organisations have endorsed it:

www.ncmd.co.uk

www.mla.gov.uk

www.cla.org.uk

www.detectorists.net
www.fid.newbury.net

www.rcahmw.gov.uk

www.britarch.ac.uk

www.nmgw.ac.uk

www.socmusarch.org.uk

www.finds.org.uk

www.nfuonline.com

ENGLISH HERITAGE
www.english-heritage.org.uk

THE BRITISH MUSEUM
www.thebritishmuseum.ac.uk

The National Council for Metal Detecting Code of Conduct

1. Do not trespass. Obtain permission before venturing on to any land.

2. Respect the Country Code. Do not leave gates open, and do not damage crops or frighten animals.

3. Wherever the site, do not leave a mess or an unsafe surface for those who may follow. It is perfectly simple to extract a coin or other small object buried a few inches below the ground without digging a great hole. Use a suitable digging implement to cut a neat flap (do not remove the plug of earth entirely from the ground)*, extract the object, reinstate the grass, sand or soil carefully, and even you will have difficulty in locating the find spot again.

4. If you discover any live ammunition or any lethal object such as an unexploded bomb or mine, do not disturb it. Mark the site carefully and report the find to the local police and landowner.

5. Help keep Britain tidy. Safely dispose of refuse you come across.

6. Report all unusual historical finds to the landowner, and acquaint yourself with current NCMD policy relating to the Voluntary Reporting of Portable Antiquities.

7. Remember it is illegal for anyone to use a metal detector on a protected area (e.g. scheduled archaeological site, SSSI, or Ministry of Defence property) without permission from the appropriate authority.

8. Acquaint yourself with the definitions of Treasure contained in the Treasure Act 1996 and its associated Code of Practice, making sure you understand your responsibilities.

9. Remember that when you are out with your metal detector you are an ambassador for our hobby. Do nothing that might give it a bad name.

10. Never miss an opportunity to explain your hobby to anyone who asks about it.

*This method of find extraction from grassland is debated by the Sports Turf Research Institute (see chapter: PUBLIC LAND) who recommend the method I have given in the INTRODUCTION.

10 SEARCH AGREEMENTS

As money will probably be involved at some time during your searches, and disputes often arise over money, I advise you to try and get a signed, written search agreement at the outset. I have to say that landowners tend not to want to get involved with such things and I have only once succeeded in getting one drawn up myself. However, the written request for permission just outlined, includes an offer to share the proceeds equally. I don't pretend to be a lawyer but I am fairly sure that, in the event of a dispute, the copy of your letter you have kept together with any written permission from the landowner would stand up as evidence of an agreement. I am sure I don't need to tell you to play fair with landowners, for their goodwill is essential to the pursuit of your hobby.

In case you can get a landowner to sign an agreement, on the following page there is an example you may copy and use:

LANDOWNER/SEARCHER AGREEMENT

The following terms and conditions are agreed between landowner and searcher:

The landowner grants permission to the searcher to use location equipment and hand tools to search and extract finds from the ground of land known as:..
....

During the period: **From**..........................**To**..............................

The searcher enters the land at the searcher's own risk.

The searcher shall report all worthwhile finds to the landowner within a reasonable time of being found in accordance with the landowner's wishes.

The searcher shall report any bombs, missiles, live ammunition or human remains discovered, to the landowner and to the police.

Archaeological discoveries will be reported to the landowner in the first instance. The information will then be passed on to the Portable Antiquities Scheme, local museum or archaeological body providing the landowner agrees.

Potential treasure discoveries will be reported to the landowner in the first instance providing this can be achieved within fourteen days. In any event the Coroner will be informed within fourteen days as prescribed by The Treasure Act.

All finds (or the value thereof) and treasure awards will be shared equally between the searcher and landowner.

The searcher shall take great care to: work tidily, avoid hindrance to the working of the land and avoid damage to the landowner's, property, animals or crops. In the unlikely event of damage the searcher shall rectify the damage at the searcher's own expense.

The searcher shall comply with any special conditions, recorded overleaf.

This agreement may be terminated by the landowner at any time and if so terminated the searcher shall immediately cease all operations.

SEARCHER	LANDOWNER
SIGNATURE:.................	....
NAME:	....
ADDRESS:	.. ..
....	....
.. ..	....
DATE:	....

11 VISITING CARDS

It is well worthwhile having cards printed or you can print some yourself from a personal computer. Not only does it show you are who you say you are when visiting a landowner for the first time but also you can leave your card so you can be contacted later. Your card can simply show your name address and telephone number, however it would be better if you can make it memorable in some way. I like a hobby related illustration on the front and an advertisement for a search and recovery service on the back. That way you have more possibility of getting permissions in the future. Here's an example:

12 PUBLIC LAND

There used to be a view in the hobby that you were generally free to detect on public open spaces like parks and commons and public rights of way such as footpaths. While you may get away with it in some areas, there has been a High Court Ruling that councils own the land for the benefit of the public, which effectively means that you should seek permission from the relevant council to use a metal detector on public land. The ruling came about through a guy called Ian Fletcher who found a gold Tudor cloak pin in a public park. The cloak pin, valued at £35000, was declared Treasure Trove (1993) and returned to the finder. The council promptly declared it was theirs, however Ian Fletcher refused to hand it over and they took him to court. The County Court ruled that the council was only custodian and the public owned the land, which meant Ian Fletcher could keep the find. The council then took the case to the High Court, which overturned the County Court ruling with the result that Ian Fletcher not only lost the cloak pin but had to pay costs as well.

You can discover what parks and open spaces exist in your area, together with the contact details of the responsible local council department, from your local library or tourist information office. This information can be found online at: http://local.direct.gov.uk/LDGRedirect/index.jsp?LGSL=461&LGI L=8&ServiceName=Find%20out%20about%20local%20parks/

Bridleways, Footpaths and Public Rights of Way are usually owned by the landowner of the land, which the way crosses. Where the way is fenced off from surrounding land the relevant highway authority: county or borough council, unitary authority or National Park authority often owns it and that would usually include roadside verges. The highway authority also has a statutory duty to keep all rights of way open and will certainly talk to the landowner if they receive complaints that your activities are in any way interfering with anyone's rights of free passage, so be careful!

Highway authorities contact details will be found at libraries and tourist information and online at the County Council (or similar administrative area) website.

Dealing with local government bureaucracy is fraught with difficulties and is not an experience for the faint hearted, so ensure, as best as you can, that the public places you want to search will be worth the effort. You may find the following booklet and articles helpful reading before you get into lengthy correspondence with your local council or highways authority.

Edward Fletcher, *The Permission Producer, How to get a YES wherever you want to use your Detector,* (Ipswich, 1998).

Edward Fletcher, 'Give Us Back Our Amenity Grass', in *Treasure Hunting,* (June, 1996). This article reviews the report from the Sports Turf Research Institute and is a good defence for the excuse that metal detecting causes excessive damage to grass. The crux of the report runs as follows:

"In my opinion as a professional Turfgrass Agronomist, I do feel that metal detecting, with due care and sufficient responsibility given, should not cause more than minor damage to the surface. Lifting of turf during moist ground conditions should not kill the sward and may indeed encourage deeper and stronger rooting. If one compares metal detecting with the various sporting activities that we at the Sports Turf Research Institute are constantly involved with, I would suggest that the lifting and replacement of turf during detecting and searching for target objects is possibly less damaging than the routine wear and tear experienced during reasonable ground and climatic conditions while playing impromptu ball games, tug-of-war, etc. on amenity grassland. With deteriorating weather conditions, the degree of damage experienced on amenity grassland during the playing of such games would be considerably more detrimental, requiring larger scale renovation works then would the one or two instances of damage created by metal detecting."

R C Spanswick, 'Metal Detecting on "Council" Land', in *Treasure Hunting,* (September, 1997); 'Further Adventures With The Council', in *Treasure Hunting,* (November, 1997)

Back issues of *Treasure Hunting* may be available from the publisher: Greenlight Publishing, The Publishing House, 119 Newland Street, Witham, Essex CM8 1WF. Email: info@treasurehunting.co.uk/ or try Ebay.

If all else fails I may be able to provide single copies of any of the articles for personal use only (not the booklet, which is available from metal detector retailers).

In addition to reviewing the above articles you will stand a much better chance of succeeding if you can claim most or all of the following:

* You are carrying out a specific project, preferably in a defined area. (See chapter: **THE PROJECT APPROACH**).

* You live and presumably pay council tax in the council's area.

* You have NCMD or FID public liability insurance.

* You have knowledge and evidence of the council consenting to activities, more harmful than metal detecting, on amenity grassland: games, sports, funfairs, bonfires, horse-riding etc.

* You have knowledge and evidence of other members of the public taking issue with the council over activities in public open spaces.

An opening gambit model letter is given on the next page. You are unlikely to get a positive reply to your first letter. To win against officialdom you need to take the moral high-ground and keep responding with calm reasoned arguments and supporting evidence for your case. It might become a war of attrition but you stand a good chance of succeeding.

What are you paying your council tax for when they won't allow you to indulge in your harmless pastime? Why can anybody do almost anything else in the park without even asking? Why do they allow the funfair to drive huge lorries onto the park? Why do they allow the boy-scouts to have bonfires? If they say it's for charity, offer to give your decimal finds to charity. If they say they have a bylaw against metal detecting, ask for the documentation and the reason for the bylaw. The council can give exemptions from bylaws – guide dogs for the blind are usually exempted from dog bylaws, for instance.

David Villanueva
2 Darn Close
Whitstable
Kent AB1 2CD
Tel: 0123 456789

Monday, 13 March 2017

Mr. E Field
Parks and Open Spaces
Somewhere City Council
Anyold Road
Somewhere
AB1 2CD

Dear Mr. Field,

THE BANDSTAND, ANYOLD PARK

I am an amateur local historian with a keen interest in the history of Somewhere.

You may know that there used to be a bandstand in Anyold Park which, according to a prominent local historian was built before 1914 and has long since disappeared. The 1938 OS 6" map shows the bandstand around the middle of the park. (OS OQ116673)

I would like to carry out a metal detector survey in this area of the park in order to confirm the site of the bandstand and to assess its popularity during its existence from datable coin and artefact losses. I assure you that the very minor disturbance of the turf that this will involve will be carried out very carefully and in line with the recommendations of the Sports Turf Research Institute 1996 report on metal detecting on amenity grassland.

I would be grateful for your consent to proceed.

Yours sincerely,

David Villanueva

Enc: SAE, Code of Practice

13 THE BLANKET APPROACH

If you send enough letters to enough farmers and landowners eventually someone will give you permission. Like any other direct mail campaign it's just a numbers game. Direct mail response is reckoned to be around 1-2%; you send out 100 letters and get one or two favourable replies. With metal detecting permission requests the response tends to be somewhat higher because you are not actually asking the recipient to part with his or her money, as such. A very enthusiastic metal detectorist of my acquaintance sent out 250 letters and got permission on seven farms, which is around 3% conversion rate. This is one way of obtaining search permissions although the amount and quality of the resulting land is very much a lottery and much of the land may be where self-respecting detectorists fear to tread. But it can work both ways, as no one knows what might be buried out there you could stumble upon a fantastic site producing finds beyond the dreams of avarice.

If you want to use this approach you can obtain a better return by writing to lesser known landowners who aren't listed in Yellow Pages (www.yell.com/) or classified telephone directories (www.192.com/). Instead, you could try trawling the ordinary telephone directory for names having farmer as their occupation or, better still trawl the electoral register at the council offices. Either way you can build up a database of names who have received little attention from other detectorists.

Another way of improving your conversion rate is to write a better letter. Quite a few years ago, Ted Fletcher produced a cheap and cheerful booklet called: *PLEASE MAY I FIELDWALK ON YOUR FARM? A brief description of MODERN FIELDWALKING and what the benefits to YOUR FARM might be if you allow me to enjoy my hobby on your fields when they are not in crop.* This briefly described a number of aspects of the hobby relevant to farmers and the idea is that you send the booklet out to a farmer of your choice who may then give you metal detecting permission. If he doesn't, then you hopefully recover the possibly tea-stained booklet and try again with another farmer. The content is very good and the fact that the booklet is still available may mean that it works, although I don't know how well. It is written for the individual and if the lazy way to detecting permission appeals to you by all means try it. I would suggest that if you get the booklet back in a scruffy state, you don't send the scruffy booklet out to another farmer. Ted Fletcher has written two complementary booklets with the idea of reversing negative responses and making best use of positive responses. They are: *Never take No Fieldwalking as the final word down on the farm* and *YES, YOU MAY FIELDWALK ON THE FARM ALL THE YEAR ROUND.*

As an individual detectorist I never use the blanket approach, however as I said earlier I was charged with finding land for a metal detecting club and I started off with the blanket approach. Basically I re-wrote *PLEASE MAY I FIELDWALK ON YOUR FARM?* In letter format, customised to suit a request for club permission. I also revised the information to suit our area and added anecdotes specific to the club. This actually resulted in an eleven-page letter, so I added a summary letter based on the back summary page of *PLEASE MAY I FIELDWALK ON YOUR FARM?* the letter achieved a better than 3% conversion rate so this should work quite well for any group of detectorists, whether a club or a few mates.

14 THE PROJECT APPROACH

I believe the most successful route to gaining permission is research based. Find a local history project to carry out, research it and then take your research to the landowner and ask permission to carry out a survey.

The scope of local history projects is enormous – you can research almost anything ancient or modern. The best type of sites to research however, are those I call continuous sites such as parishes, track-ways and watercourses, which cover several tracts of land. The reason is that once you get a foothold it is much easier to gain permission to search neighbouring land and so one project can keep you going for years.

There are many other projects that make excellent detecting sites and what you choose really depends on what your interests are and what exists in your locality. You really want to look for sites where people lived, worked or played in the past, preferably in large numbers. The sites I have found particularly interesting and rewarding, in addition to the continuous sites, are: fairs, hop-picking, hundred courts, manor houses, markets, mills and sports sites.

While the value of research has been discussed since the hobby began, very little had been written on how to carry out research until I wrote *Site Research for Detectorists, Fieldwalkers & Archaeologists,* (Greenlight Publishing, 2006). I'll let the publisher and others speak for me on the book:

Site research, it seems, is one of the more neglected aspects of our hobby. Why should one field be productive of finds year after year and yet the next field be totally barren? The answer is past human activity, and David Villanueva shows in this book simple ways, through map and document research, how to locate such activity. The methods are clearly explained and often require no more than an hour or two spent at the local library or on the Internet.

And, as an added bonus, farmers are far more likely to grant search permission if an approach is made to them armed with documents detailing the past history of their land. In fact, one chapter of the book is devoted to ways of gaining land to search.

Site Research contains 160 full colour pages divided into 20 chapters, profusely illustrated with examples of maps and documents, and examples of finds resulting from the suggested research methods. Although written mainly for detectorists, this book will also be of interest and help to fieldwalkers, local historians and archaeologists.

David Villanueva has over 30 years of experience in metal detecting and research, and is a regular contributor to *Treasure*

Hunting magazine. He has been responsible for several reported finds of Treasure, and has built up a collection of other coins and artefacts that would be the envy of many.

Whether you are a beginner or an experienced detectorist, within a short while of owning this book and applying its lessons, you will start to acquire more productive sites and as a result start to make better finds.

Chapter titles: * Using Archives, Libraries & Computers * County Maps * Ordnance Survey Maps * Practical Map Reading * Town Plans * Road Maps * Road, River, Canal & Railway Construction Maps * Enclosure & Tithe Maps * Estate Maps * Sea Charts * Aerial Photographs, Maps & Surveys * Local Histories * Guide to County Histories * Domesday Book * Gaining Search Permission * Search Agreements * Living with the Treasure Act * Code of Practice * Bibliography & Sources

Greenlight Publishing: 250mm x 190mm, 160 pages, £20.00 post free ISBN 1 897738 285

"I have enjoyed working on this book and feel that I have personally learnt a lot from it, even though I purchased my first metal detector in 1971 and have been in the hobby for many years."

Greg Payne, Editor

"I have just received my copy of the new book Site Research by David Villanueva. This book is a cracker for all of us as the longer that I am in this hobby the more I have a thirst for more data. The new folks to the hobby will find it's a way to advance their knowledge in a short time. The illustrations are on a par with Benet's [a superb colour finds catalogue] and there is an insight when it comes to doing the homework prior to going on a dig is a must. Computer sites for data are also included and pictures of old maps from centuries past are very interesting. Well I think that I have said enough to wet the appetite of those who want to get the best out of the hobby. It certainly won't break the bank at £20 and there is always the Xmas list."

JBM, Bristol

So if you want to learn how to research for metal detecting, you need this book. It is available from me at True Treasure Books (www.trutreasurebooks.net/), Greenlight Publishing, metal detector retailers and booksellers.

On the next page is a letter for a typical project:

www.swalemdc.org.uk

2 Darn Close
Whitstable
Kent
AB1 2CD

Tel: 0123 456789

Mobile: 07760 195883

E-mail: david@truetreasurebooks.net

29 December 2006

O MacDonald & Sons
Eieio Farm
Anywhere
AB1 2CD

Dear Mr. Macdonald,

SALT WAY PROJECT

As you have land lying between the coast and
City, you have probably heard of the *Salt Way*
or *Salt Road,* which is supposed to have existed
from ancient times to facilitate the transport
of valuable salt, fish and other goods to the
City. Several local historians have discussed
the *Salt Way* and its possible routes and
although there are early references of material
being transported from coast to City there
appear to be no records of the actual route.
The local history website, *Here's History Kent*
(http://www.hereshistorykent.org.uk/) has
recently identified: "*the origins and
development of a trackway from the coast to*

City" as a key research project for the area.

For conventional archaeology, trackways are extremely difficult to investigate, unless they are metalled (and if the *Salt Way* was metalled we'd probably know by now), because there are no remains to dig and very little visible evidence is left for traditional fieldwalkers to find. Also the nature of trackways is that they would often be diverted when ground conditions caused difficulties, with the result that over time they covered a swathe of land perhaps 200-300 yards or metres wide. To fieldwalkers with metal detectors, however, trackways are an easy feature to investigate. Past users of the trackway would have dropped a multitude of small metal objects, such as coins, buttons and buckles, which can be recovered, dated and plotted to reveal the course of the trackway in various historical periods. (By way of illustration, there are two metal detecting articles on similar trackways appended.)

As keen outdoor local historians, which is how we describe ourselves and our hobby, we are very interested in investigating the course of the *Salt Way* and would be grateful if you would give permission for us to undertake a metal detector search on your land. We would only undertake a search when land is free of crops and would strictly limit numbers of searchers to your preference and the land area available. We assure you that we will share all finds equally (i.e. 50% to you and 50% to the club) and that we will respect your wishes if you have a particular collecting interest in some of the items we show you at the end of a search.

Every club member recognises that our first duty is to the landowner / occupier and adheres to the enclosed code of practice as far as possible. Any consulting with third parties or publication is only carried out with the landowner / occupier's express permission. In addition every club member carries NFU approved civil liability insurance up to £10,000,000 indemnity, in the highly unlikely event of a claim. The hobby is very proud of the fact that in some 30 years that this insurance has been employed, there has NEVER been a claim.

We look forward to your kind reply (SAE enclosed).

Best wishes,

David Villanueva

David Villanueva

(Chairman)

PS: If any artefacts over 300 years old have already been found on you land, we would greatly appreciate any information you can give us. Again this information would not be divulged to anyone else without your consent.

Enclosures: Code of Practice for Responsible Metal Detecting

'Ways of Old' (*Treasure Hunting*, November 2003)

'A Canterbury Tale' (*The Searcher*, January 2004)

SAE

I appreciate that most of you will not have written articles you can include, however sending copies of relevant articles is an excellent way of showing the landowner what you are trying to achieve and improving your chances of gaining permission. So you really need to find a suitable article from one of the metal detecting magazines, which you can copy. Strictly speaking you should ask the magazine for permission before making copies, however I am quite happy for you to use any of my articles listed below. If you have the particular magazine issue, just copy the article, otherwise you can contact me at True Treasure Books for a copy (free by email or £1 per article by post).

'To the Manor Drawn' (*The Searcher,* January and March, 1997). Searching a deserted medieval manor house site.

'A Riparian Tale' (*The Searcher,* May 1999). Finds along a river bank.

'Another Day, Another Manor' (*The Searcher,* April 2000). Finds from another deserted medieval manor house site.

'Gold for the Gods' (*The Searcher,* November 2000). Finding a scattered hoard of gold staters on a river site.

'Gathering in the Past' (*The Searcher,* September 2001) Finds from a hundred meeting or court site.

'Deserted Medieval Manors' (*Treasure Hunting,* December 2001). Rewrite and combination of two deserted manor sites.

'Trading Places' (*Treasure Hunting,* May 2002). Searching medieval market and fair sites.

'Find of the Day' (*The Searcher,* December 2002). The finding of a medieval gold iconographic ring in the grounds of a manor house.

'Mills of Gold' (*Treasure Hunting,* May 2003). Finding & searching water-mill sites.

'Ways of Old' (*Treasure Hunting,* November 2003). Searching Roman roads.

'A Canterbury Tale' (*The Searcher,* January 2004). Searching the Pilgrims Way (medieval tracks).

'Enclosures, Tithes & The Maidens' Race' (*Treasure Hunting,* April 2005). History of Tithe & Enclosure maps, illustrated with the story of a 350 year-old running race.

'Noble Quest' (*Treasure Hunting,* December 2005). The search for hammered gold on manor sites.

'Hopping for More Finds' (*Treasure Hunting,* September 2006). A short history of hop-picking in Britain and finds made on hop-farms.

As an alternative, my book, *Site Research*, discussed earlier, covers a similar range of sites in a number of case studies, which you can copy and use to gain search permission on similar sites.

15 ON THE MOVE

There is an opportunity to gain search permission from people moving home, whether that home is a house, farm or estate. If someone is leaving they may be less bothered about having metal detectorists searching their land and quite interested in having any lost possessions found or a possible windfall before they leave. Similarly if they decline your offer, their buyer may be interested in your proposition, so you have two chances. People on the move are very easy to find as their intention is well advertised and what's more, gardens, particularly old gardens, make excellent metal detecting sites owing to the concentration of many losses in a relatively small area. Any property with a garden would do but properties, particularly older properties, with an acre or more of land would be better.

To find property for sale is a fairly simple matter, you can look in the property pages of your local newspapers; estate agents windows or search online for land or property for sale. In some cases the name and address of the vendor will be given but you will get a reasonably accurate location, short of asking the agent for full details. The agent probably won't give you full details unless you register as a buyer, which I would avoid for this purpose as it may cause you problems if you become a genuine potential property buyer. However, with the location details you can drive, cycle or walk around the relevant area and deliver your message when you spot the inevitable 'For Sale' board.

On the next page is the message, which can take the form of a letter or a leaflet:

www.swalemdc.org.uk

2 Darn Close
Whitstable
Kent
AB1 2CD

Tel: 0123 456789

Mobile: 07760 195883

E-mail: david@truetreasurebooks.net

Monday, 13 March 2017

WHAT WILL YOU BE LEAVING BEHIND WHEN YOU MOVE?

Have you lost any valuable metal object in your grounds? Jewellery or a family heirloom perhaps? Even objects lost within your home may have become buried in your grounds, perhaps taken there by a child, a bird or an animal.

Who knows what previous occupiers of your home have lost or even deliberately buried in your garden and before the present house was built any number of people, going back 3000 years, could have deposited their metal valuables in your land! A single coin could be worth hundreds of thousands of pounds (e.g. 14th century gold Double Leopard, £400,000) and a single artefact several million pounds (e.g. Middleham 15th century gold and sapphire pendant, £2,500,000), not to mention the possibility of hoards or caches!

The record of valuable finds from gardens is growing daily. Just a few examples are:

57

* An Iron Age gold necklace (£90,000), Suffolk

* An Anglo-Saxon gold cross (£50,000), Kent

* £563 in 20th century silver coins in a biscuit tin (£2500), Worcestershire

* A 15th century gold ring, (£4000), Kent

* 120 gold 14th century coins in a pot, (£100,000), Kent

As experienced metal detectorists we can help ensure you leave little behind unintentionally. You have our firm assurance that we will:

* Carry out a free metal detector survey of your grounds.

* Restore all your personal property to you.

* Share any other finds or treasure awards equally with you.

* Work tidily without leaving a mess and remove all junk uncovered.

* Respect your property and take care to avoid causing damage, loss or hindrance (we have approved Public Liability Insurance).

Contact us today and you could not only recover your lost valuables but also gain a windfall that might pay your moving expenses or even buy your next property. What have you got to lose?

Best wishes,

David Villanueva

David Villanueva (Chairman)

PS. We appreciate that you may not wish to use our services at this busy time. In that case, we would be grateful if you will kindly pass this letter on to your purchaser.

Enc. SAE, *Find of the Day* (published article)

16 THE SERVICES OFFER

Apart from the services you can offer with a metal detector, such as lost key, jewellery, tool and tractor parts recovery and pipe and cable locating, you can also offer your labour in return for detecting permission. This will appeal to many small farmers who have few resources but perhaps plenty of land. As an example, a farmer I know tried to level a heavily rutted footpath by having a cultivator run over it. That operation levelled out the ruts but left large lumps of turf all over the path. Seeing the walkers negotiate it was like watching the Olympic 100 metre hurdles. Clearly the farmer needed to sort the path out quickly before someone complained to the Highways Authority but when he had retired and rented his land out, he had sold all his farm machinery and didn't have the tools to deal with the clearance task. I offered to bring a few lads over from the club to clear the path, which was gratefully accepted with the offer of a 70-acre field to use afterwards. Seven of us completed the job in two hours and we spent the rest of the day detecting.

As well as farms there are plenty of opportunities for accessing other types of sites through various volunteer projects. Your local council probably produces a magazine or newsletter (try an online search for council name + magazine), which will undoubtedly contain details of volunteer projects on land such as clearing litter, overgrown vegetation and other reclamation activities. Such events will probably also be advertised in your local newspaper, as there will always be more work than volunteers. While it would be difficult to demand that you be allowed to use your metal detector on such projects after the event, a polite request should be viewed sympathetically.

There is also a network of volunteer bureaux who co-ordinate volunteers to, amongst other services, undertake gardening for the elderly and infirm. Again you can do the community a favour while providing yourself with plenty of opportunity for gaining metal detecting permissions. Remember your reputation will get around by performing this service and you should get plenty of offers of other land to detect on, even farmland perhaps if one of your clients is well connected.

Finally there are local and national recovery groups such as the Waterway Recovery Group, PO Box 114, Rickmansworth, WD3 1ZY. Tel: 01923 711114. Email: enquiries@wrg.org.uk/ https://www.waterways.org.uk/wrg/ who organise events throughout the main holiday periods, restoring derelict canals. You would have to pick your project here to result in dredgings, spoil heaps or cleared towpaths to provide an opportunity for detecting. Projects like building a bridge or new lock, for instance, wouldn't allow much scope.

The Countryside Restoration Trust, Barton, Cambridge, CB3 7AG http://www.livingcountryside.org.uk/volunteer.htm/ Tel: 01223 262999 is another possibility and there is a large list of voluntary, campaigning and social organisations on the Ramblers Association website: http://www.ramblers.org.uk/ (Ramblers' Association main office, 2nd Floor Camelford House, 87-90 Albert Embankment, London SE1 7TW, UK Tel: 020 7339 8500.)

17 THE SUBSIDY APPROACH

I've left this one until last as it will usually mean that you have to part with your money in exchange for detecting permission and generally you will need to be part of a group of detectorists. I have heard of some landowners who will let you pay £5-£10 and go detecting for the day on your own. Also Bob Bailey used to produce a book called *Metal Detecting Farm Holiday Guide,* later *British Farm Holidays,* which listed several hundred farms throughout the UK that allowed metal detecting providing you paid for the accommodation and originally you could pay a fee for the day, without the accommodation. The book seems to have ceased and the farms will probably have been well detected anyway, nevertheless if you are taking a country holiday you may be able to organise detecting permission where you stay.

Because the sum offered becomes more attractive with larger numbers, this approach works best with a group, either formal as in a club or informal as a number of individual detectorists you can attract. You could take an entrepreneurial approach here too, like *Weekend Wanderers*, who organise digs in the Home Counties, and charge either an annual subscription or 20% of the daily fee to detectorists taking part. The actual sum you offer depends on a number of factors such as the location and the number of detectorists involved. I have heard it work with as little as £2 per head per day but I think £5 - £10 per head per day is more realistic. In terms of land area you need ½ - 1 acre (¼ - ½ hectare) per detectorist per day to make it worthwhile although you can always put on a half-day dig with less land. If you are going to use this approach regularly I would advise doing some basic research on the land first, else if nobody finds anything your detectorists will whinge and whine and withdraw their support from future events or rallies.

So if we take the payment as £10 per head per day in round figures, the options are as follows:

RALLY	DETECTORISTS	ACRES*	PAYMENT
Local (half-day)	10-20	5+	£50-£100
Local (full-day)	10-20	10+	£100-£200
County	50-100	50+	£500-£1000
National (1-day)	500-1000	500+	£5000-£10000
National (2-day)	500-1000	1000+	£10000-£20000
National (3-day)	500-1000	1500+	£20000-£30000

*Numbers of detectorists can always be limited to accommodate a lower acreage, so for instance a national 1-day rally could be limited to 500 detectorists on 250 acres and any rallies could be repeated a number of times providing land (even the same land) is available.

Rally-goers will appreciate that the fee charged for County and National rallies are higher, however expenses increase as the rally gets larger. A local rally should have only nominal expenses, however County and National rallies will require the hiring of portable toilets and advertising expenditure. To offset that there may be catering and other sales concessions and overnight camping fees. If the rally is being organised on behalf of a charity then a raffle can be held for increased funds and the charity may be able to reduce some of the expenditure by negotiating free advertising or free toilet facilities.

Larger rallies with more than 50 detectorists attending will need to be organised carefully. Consideration needs to be given to public event management, health and safety, licensing and recording of finds. If any of the land is under Stewardship, then Natural England will need to be informed at least 12 weeks in advance and finds recording may be compulsory. See the PAS guide: https://finds.org.uk/getinvolved/guides/rallycode/

Landowners can be approached by letter or leaflet (at farmer's markets, county shows, ploughing matches, etc.), along the following lines:

www.swalemdc.org.uk

2 Darn Close
Whitstable
Kent
AB1 2CD

Tel: 0123 456789

Mobile: 07760 195883

E-mail: david@truetreasurebooks.net

NEW FARMING SUBSIDY

Whenever you plough, cultivate, harvest or mow, you can now benefit from an additional payment.

Local history enthusiasts are keen to pay you money if you allow them to search your crop-free land with a metal detector. Depending on the acreage available and how many people you are prepared to accommodate at any one time this payment can range from around £50 to over £30,000. In addition there could be a further substantial payment if treasure or other valuable objects are discovered – for example the reward for the Hoxne hoard was £1.75 million. Of course, if you are not interested in the money yourself, your favourite charity could always benefit.

Here's the offer. All you have to do is

supply land free of crops and generally with
either a bare surface or vegetation no more
then about three inches high (we can work
around trees). For larger events we may need
help with land for parking and overnight
camping (for extra payment). We will carry out
all necessary organisation, leave your land
tidy and pay you around £10 per head per day.
The following table shows examples of what is
achievable:

RALLY	DETECTORISTS	ACRES*	PAYMENT
Local (half-day)	10-20	5+	£50-£100
Local (full-day)	10-20	10+	£100-£200
County	50-100	50+	£500-£1000
National (1-day)	500-1000	500+	£5000-£10000
National (2-day)	500-1000	1000+	£10000-£20000
National (3-day)	500-1000	1500+	£20000-£30000

*Numbers of detectorists can always be
limited to accommodate a lower acreage, so for
instance a national one-day event could be
limited to 500 detectorists on 250 acres and
any events could be repeated a number of times
providing land (even the same land) is
available.

The fee charged to detectorists for County
and National events are higher than local
events, however expenses increase as the event
gets larger. A local event should have only
nominal expenses, however County and National
events will require the hiring of portable
toilets and advertising expenditure. To offset
that there may be catering and other sales
concessions and overnight camping fees. If the
event is being organised on behalf of a charity
then a raffle can be held for increased funds
and the charity may be able to reduce some of
the expenditure by negotiating free advertising
or free toilet facilities.

I would be delighted to discuss the matter
further with you.

Best wishes,

David Villanueva

David Villanueva (Chairman)

18 BIBLIOGRAPHY AND FURTHER READING

Fletcher, Edward, *Never take No Fieldwalking as the final word down on the farm,* (1998); *Please May I Fieldwalk on Your Farm?* (1997); *Please May I Research The History of Your Farm,* (1998); *The Permission Producer,* (1998); *Yes, You May Fieldwalk on The Farm,* (1998)

Kahn, John Ellison, Dphil, Ed., *How to Write and Speak Better,* (Reader's Digest, 1991)

Villanueva, David, *Metal Detecting, Genealogy and Family History,* (True Treasure Books, 2006); *Site Research for Detectorists, Fieldwalkers & Archaeologists,* (Greenlight Publishing, 2006); *The Successful Treasure Hunter's Essential Dowsing Manual,* (True Treasure Books, 2005)

MAGAZINES

The Searcher, 17 Down Road, Merrow, Guildford, Surrey, GU1 2PX. Tel: 01483 830133, Email: info@thesearcher.co.uk/ Web: www.thesearcher.co.uk/

Treasure Hunting, Greenlight Publishing, The Publishing House, 119 Newland Street, Witham, Essex, CM8 1WF. Tel: 01376 521900, Email: info@treasurehunting.co.uk/ Web: www.treasurehunting.co.uk/

19 APPENDIX – MAJOR UK LANDOWNERS

Church Estates Commissioners

No 1 Millbank, London. Tel: 020 7898 1000.
http://www.cofe.anglican.org/

The Crown Estate

16 New Burlington Place (England, Northern Ireland, Wales),
London, W1S 2HX. Email: enquiries@thecrownestate.co.uk/
http://www.thecrownestate.co.uk/mh_metal_detecting/

Forestry Commission GB and Scotland

Silvan House, 231 Corstorphine Road, Edinburgh,Scotland,
EH12 7AT. Telephone: 0131 334 0303 (switchboard). Enquiries:
0845 FORESTS (3673787). Fax: 0131 334 3047. E-mail:
enquiries@forestry.gsi.gov.uk/ Web: http://www.forestry.gov.uk/

Ministry of Defence

The Defence Estate Access and Recreation Officer contact:
Richard Brooks, Defence Estates, Land Warfare Centre,
Warminster, Wiltshire, BA12 0DJ. Telephone: 01985 222913.
Email: richard.brooks@de.mod.uk/ Web: http://www.mod.uk/

The National Trust

PO Box 39, Warrington, WA5 7WD. Tel: 0870 458 4000.
Fax: 020 8466 6824. Email: enquiries@thenationaltrust.org.uk/
http://www.thenationaltrust.org.uk/

The Port of London Authority

Marine Administrative Support, (Foreshore Permits), London River House, Royal Pier Road, Gravesend, Kent, DA12 2BG. Tel: 01474562339. http://www.portoflondon.co.uk/

Royal Society for the Protection of Birds

The Lodge, Sandy, Bedfordshire, SG19 2DL. Tel: 01767 680551. www.rspb.org.uk/

SOURCES FOR LAND OWNERSHIP IN SCOTLAND

Church of Scotland General Trustees

Own a number of properties including a large number of small areas of land.

Contact: Church of Scotland General Trustees, 121 George Street, Edinburgh, EH2 4YN Tel: 0131 225 5722. www.churchofscotland.org.uk/

The Crown Estate

The Commissioners own five rural estates at Glenlivet, Fochabers, Applegirth, Stirling and Whitehill.

Contact: The Crown Estate, 6 Bells Brae, Edinburgh, EH4 3BJ. Tel: 0131 260 6070. www.thecrownestate.co.uk/

Forestry Commission

Website contains names and addresses of the local Forest Enterprise district offices which hold local information about the Commission's land holdings.

Contact: 231 Corstorphine Road, Edinburgh, EH12 7AT. Tel: 0131 334 0303. Fax: 0131 314 6152. www.forestry.gov.uk/

John Muir Trust

Contact: 41 Commercial Street, Leith, Edinburgh, EH6 6JD. Tel: 0131 554 0114. Fax: 0131 555 2112. www.jmt.org/

Ministry of Defence

Website gives details of Ministry of Defence Estates contacts in Scotland.

Contact: DE Rosyth, 30 Hilton Road, Rosyth, Fife, KY11 2BL. Tel: 01383 648020. Fax: 01383 648080. www.mod.uk/

The National Trust for Scotland

Website contains a list of Trust properties.

Contact: Wemyss House, 28 Charlotte Square, Edinburgh, EH2 4ET. Tel: 0131 243 9300. Fax: 0131 248 9301.
E-mail: information@nts.org.uk/ Web: www.nts.org.uk/

Royal Society for the Protection of Birds

Website gives details of the Society's reserves in Scotland.

Contact: Dunedin House, 25 Ravelston Terrace, Edinburgh, EH4 3TP. Tel: 0131 311 6500. Fax: 0131 311 6569. www.rspb.org.uk/

Scottish Executive Environment and Rural Affairs Department; Scottish Ministers Crofting Estates

SEERAD administers estates extending to some 104,000 hectares on behalf of Scottish Ministers. About 99% of the total area is croft land in the highland and island areas of Scotland.

Contact: SEERAD Estate Management Branch, Pentland House, 47 Robb's Loan, Edinburgh, EH14 1TY. Tel: 0131 244 6286. www.scotland.gov.uk/

Scottish Rural Property and Business Association

Represents ownership and management of rural land in Scotland.

Contact: Stuart House, Eskmills Business Park, Musselburgh, EH21 7PB. Tel: 0131 653 5400. Fax: 0131 653 5401.
www.srpba.com/

Scottish Natural Heritage

Website gives details of local area offices.

Contact:12 Hope Terrace, Edinburgh, EH9 2AS. Tel: 0131 447 4784. Fax: 0131 446 2277. www.snh.org.uk/

Scottish Wildlife Trust

Currently manages and owns majority of over 120 wildlife reserves covering over 22,000 hectares, spread across Scotland.

Contact: Cramond House, Cramond Glebe Road, Edinburgh, EH4 6NS. Tel: 0131 312 7765. Fax: 0131 312 8075.
www.swt.org.uk/

BOOKS IN PRINT FROM THE SAME AUTHOR

THE SUCCESSFUL TREASURE HUNTER'S SECRET MANUAL: Discovering Treasure Auras in the Digital Age, Soft Cover, 152mm x 229mm, (6 x 9 inches) 102 pages, (CreateSpace, 2017) ISBN 9781540747815

THE SUCCESSFUL TREASURE HUNTER'S SECRET MANUAL: How to Use Modern Cameras to Locate Buried Metals, Gold, Silver, Coins, Caches... (E-Book)

CLEANING COINS & ARTEFACTS: Conservation * Restoration * Presentation, Soft Cover, 210mm x 146mm, (8.25 x 5.75 inches) 110 pages, (Greenlight Publishing, 2008) ISBN 978 1 897738 337

THE SUCCESSFUL TREASURE HUNTER'S ESSENTIAL COIN AND RELIC MANAGER: How to Clean, Conserve, Display, Photograph, Repair, Restore, Replicate and Store Metal Detecting Finds (E-Book)

PERMISSION IMPOSSIBLE: Metal Detecting Search Permission Made Easy, Soft Cover, 210mm x 146mm, (8.25 x 5.75 inches) 52 pages, (True Treasure Books, 2007) ISBN 978 0 9550325 3 0 (Also an E-Book)

SITE RESEARCH FOR DETECTORISTS, FIELDWALKERS & ARCHAEOLOGISTS, Soft Cover, 250mm x 190mm, (9.75 x 7.5 inches) 160 pages, (Greenlight Publishing, 2006) ISBN 1 897738 285

THE SUCCESSFUL TREASURE HUNTER'S ESSENTIAL SITE RESEARCH MANUAL: How to Find Productive Metal Detecting Sites, (E-Book)

SUCCESSFUL DETECTING SITES: Locate 1000s of Superb Sites and Make More Finds, Soft Cover, 250mm x 190mm, (9.75 x 7.5 inches) 238 pages, (Greenlight Publishing, 2007) ISBN 978 1 897738 306

THE ESSENTIAL GUIDE TO OLD, ANTIQUE AND ANCIENT METAL SPOONS, Soft Cover, 210mm x 146mm, 88 pages, (True Treasure Books, 2008) ISBN 978 0 9550325 4 7 (Also an E-Book)

DOWSING FOR TREASURE: The New Successful Treasure Hunter's Essential Dowsing Manual, Soft Cover, 152mm x 229mm, (6 x 9 inches) 96 pages, (CreateSpace, 2016) ISBN 9781518766060 (Also an E-Book)

MY ANCESTOR LEFT AN HEIRLOOM: Discovering Heirlooms and Ancestors Through the Metalwork They Left Behind, Soft Cover, 210mm x 146mm, (8.25 x 5.75 inches) 84 pages, (True Treasure Books, 2011) ISBN 978 0 9550325 6 1.

MY ANCESTOR LEFT AN HEIRLOOM: Hunting Family History and Genealogy Treasure Through Metal Detecting Finds (E-Book)

METAL DETECTING MADE EASY: A Guide for Beginners and Reference for All, Soft Cover, 210mm x 146mm, (8.25 x 5.75 inches) 128 pages, (True Treasure Books, 2014) ISBN 978 0 9550325 7 8 (Also an E-Book)

FAITHFUL ATTRACTION: How to Drive Your Metal Detector to Find Treasure (E-Book)

TOKENS & TRADERS OF KENT in the Seventeenth, Eighteenth & Nineteenth Centuries, Soft Cover, 215mm x 140mm, (8.5 x 5.5 inches) 112 pages, (True Treasure Books, 2015) ISBN 978 0 9550325 8 5 (Also an E-Book)

METAL DETECTING BENEFITS FOR LANDOWNERS (co-authored with Jacq le Breton), Soft Cover, 152mm x 229mm, (6 x 9 inches) 32 pages, (CreateSpace, 2016) ISBN 978-1537341118 (a booklet for European metal detectorists, to give to landowners as a deluxe calling card)

ABOUT THE AUTHOR

Photo: Brian Green, with kind permission, Whitstable Times

David Villanueva was born in Birmingham, England in 1951. His mother bought him Ted Fletcher's book, *A Fortune Under Your Feet*, in 1972, which inspired him to buy a BFO metal detector. David became hooked on treasure hunting.

In 1985, a move to Kent, England saw David searching beaches with an old Pulse Induction detector. After buying a new Induction Balance detector, he joined a metal detecting club and gained permission to search a small farm, making all manner of old and interesting finds. Having a keen interest in history, David researched his locality, which led to more productive sites to search and write about in over a dozen books and the two British metal detecting magazines – *Treasure Hunting* and *The Searcher* – which have published more than thirty of David's articles.

Continually delving into local history and following up his research in the field, David suddenly found himself reporting real treasures in the form of caches of ancient tools, gold coins and Roman, Saxon and medieval precious metal jewelry. Over a dozen of David's finds have been recorded under the Treasure Act.

Printed in Great Britain
by Amazon

38165503R00045